# How To Do Spiritual Warfare The Right Way

*Increase Your Effectiveness By Winning The Battles Legally First*

By Greg Kurjata

# FOREWORD

Greg Kurjata and I have been good friends over many years and both he and and Val have blessed Shirley and myself so much in their home, at conferences and just doing life together. Together they have impacted tens of thousands of people with their online broadcasts and personal ministry.

Greg has a true, amazing gift as a seer in the body of Christ, and is able to take what he sees in the spirit and break it down so that Christians not only walk out their visions and dreams, but have a biblical mandate that manifests in real freedom and fruit. This book is not only great for the insight and revelation knowledge concerning Heavenly dynamics, it also focuses on what NOT to do when it comes to spiritual warfare, angelic visitations, etc.

I find that many intercessors, prayer warriors and and even houses of prayer may find themselves actually missing the central focus of what God has called them to, and many end up as casualties along the way, either in their homes, marriages or spiritually.

Greg will help you understand what are your first commitments to intercession and how to cooperate with God to see them come to pass. Just watching someone online or being excited because you think God has called you to a prayer ministry does not qualify you or guarantee results.

Here is where Greg can help you to shake off any misconceptions of your own prayer life and teach you to have real fruit in both your life and ministry.

We have seen and heard many testimonies of people who changed their prayer strategy after listening to Greg and Val, and saw family salvations, mighty transformations and even healings and miracles - in other people and even their own lives! And I believe this book will spur you on in your daily walk with God and revitalize your prayer life and ministry.

Get ready for an eye opening experience and expect God to change you from Glory to Glory as you read this book.

Charlie Robinson
Golden Lion Productions
President

# TABLE OF CONTENTS

---

# INTRODUCTION:
# HOW TO READ THIS BOOK

This book is in your hands for a reason.

It's not by accident.

Since you're a serious student of the Holy Spirit, you felt inspired to get this book. It might be because of feeling intimidated by evil spirits, or that you feel like you're punching blind when you go to pray in this way. Maybe spiritual warfare is something you've always wanted to learn how to do but found some of the info out there confusing.

If you're like me, then you've had many prayer failures in this space of spiritual warfare, and you want to find some answers as to why. We hope to answer many of your questions.

There's a lot of mystery around spiritual warfare that I'm going to clear up for you in this book. You'll learn practical ways and biblical strategies that you may not have been aware of up until now.

The exciting thing is that you can learn them.

And they are effective.

There's two things that will happen with this book.

First of all, you're going to learn how to do spiritual warfare through the Courts Of Heaven. If you don't know anything yet about the courts of heaven, this will be an introduction for you. You'll get the very best teaching that we have available. What you learn, you can put to work right away, in fact there's a resource we will tell you about later on, that will give you the blueprint for some of the more advanced strategies we have developed over the past 15 years.

And secondly, we want you to join our community (over 50,000 strong at the time of this edit). We have helped thousands of people to improve their lives in every way imaginable through courses, challenges, and coaching. We would love to have you in our community at this stage of your journey in life.

It's a fact that even the most successful athletes, who are at the top of their game, have coaches and mentors to help them be even better. Growth does not happen in a vacuum. We all need help from those around us to be stronger and more courageous in this life.

It's our hope that by the end of this book you will see that we have nothing but your best interest at heart and are sincere in the offer to help you get to the place you want to be in terms of walking in the power and Presence of God - <u>without it getting weird or flaky</u>.

As you'll soon find out, I'm going to be fully transparent, honest, and blunt with you through the pages of this book. One of my early business mentors taught me that if you want people to believe you can help them, help them.

**So, I want to help you.**

I want to help you get results from what you read in this book. This is inspired by Genesis 13:14,

Adonai said to Abram, after Lot had moved away from him, "Look all around you **from where you are**, to the north, the south, the east and the west. 15 **All the land you see** I will give to you

You can only make progress from where you are, not where you thought you were, or from where you wished you were. Where you are is where you are. It takes a bit of humility to recognize this. And the truth is, it is possible that you are further along and better off than you thought you were.

In order to get the most out of this material you need to actually do the exercises. I heard a saying many years ago in relation to setting goals and personal transformation:

### "Don't Just Think It - Ink It"

Now, there are a couple of reasons why you want to do it in this way.

First of all it's the mind to paper connection. Your thoughts being written by your hand onto paper, causes something that's invisible to become visible. Your thoughts are the invisible portion, and as you write those thoughts out they become visible. The kinetic connection between your thoughts and the paper is what involves your entire focus and attention. The value of what you are writing increases because you have to think about it, write it down, and then read it.

Secondly, it gives you a chance to truly contemplate the change that you will want to make. Recognizing there may be a deficiency is often difficult because maybe we like to think we have it together all the time. But when you can see it written down, you're able to assess and evaluate where you are right now. It will locate you. And that is a good thing.

## HERE IS THE FIRST ASSESSMENT

Which one of the following statements is closest to your current experience with prayer?   Check one

| | |
|---|---|
| I am fairly new to the whole area of prayer and intercession | |
| I have a good understanding of intercession and spiritual warfare | |
| I pray this way all the time and want to learn more to get better results | ✓ |

Below is information about how each of these areas are served via the content of this book AND what we have available in our community to further help you.

**Fairly New:**  this book will provide you with a solid road map to safely and easily pray in a way that can change not only your life, but the lives of those you pray for.

A resource that will help you that we have available in our community is The 5 Day Salvation Challenge. This is a free training that happens **LIVE** once a month and over 80,000 (at the time of this edit) people have registered for it to date. In it you learn an effective prayer strategy using the courts of heaven, so your loved ones can come to Jesus. You can learn more about it here:  **www.5dsc.ca**

**Good Understanding:** your experience tells you that there is more to learn because of some of the road blocks that you have run up against. You've experienced backlash ; and are confused as to why that has been happening. What you learn here will show you why that happens.

A resource in our community that will help you increase your success rate in prayer is Advanced Prayer Strategies Workshop. This shows you how to deal with things like curses, blood oaths, generational trauma, etc by using a function in the courts of heaven. You may already have this, but if you don't you can learn about it here. www.jchonline.ca/advanced

All The Time: you know some things about some things, and recognize that there are different strategies that can be deployed for unique results in certain areas. You're looking for a way to be even better at praying this way. This book will add some skills to your prayer tool chest.

In our community, we have over 2,300 (at the time of this edit) students in the online course. It covers what you need to know about the courts of heaven in an easy to understand and take action kind of way. Learn more here: www.jchonline.ca/jchcourse

In the first part of the book we're going to look at different methods that are commonly used in spiritual warfare and why they have been ineffective in producing the results that we feel like they should produce. Then we're going to look at how the only way to deal with the enemy in a predictable and consistent manner is legally. This is where the courts of heaven come in. They are a heavenly mechanism available to you that enable you to obtain justice for every incidence of injustice you have experienced, plus any injustice you encounter in your relationships or community.

We're going to show many examples in scripture of leaders that God selected to carry out this kind of spiritual warfare. You'll be surprised to see how frequently this happened throughout the Scriptures. I know I was.

You'll see how Jesus used justice to completely defeat the enemy on our behalf. You'll see the thread of justice and the courts of heaven right from the beginning to the end of the Bible. It's very exciting, and very empowering to you.

**I call the courts of heaven a treasure hidden in plain sight.**

Finally, we're going to show you how to put what you learn to work right away in your own life, then in the life of those you love. From there you will extend into the broader community where you live.

This method of prayer has radically changed my life.

Before, when I would do spiritual warfare, it was like I was beating the air and shadowboxing. After the Holy Spirit showed me how the Courts Of Heaven function in relation to spiritual warfare, I was completely transformed.

I hope the same happens for you. That you feel empowered.

One time we were teaching the Courts Of Heaven in a home study group, and one of the men made this comment, "We are not powerless. The courts of heaven give us a tremendous power." The look on his face was priceless. It was a new realization for him. He was so happy because now he had a way to deal with the situations that previously caused him a lot of stress.

He had hope.

Now let's get into it.

# CHAPTER 1:

# WHY BAD STUFF STILL HAPPENS ON THE EARTH

———

## HOW TO DO SPIRITUAL WARFARE THE RIGHT WAY

BY GREG KURJATA

**Daniel 7:9-11** *(Complete Jewish Bible)*

9 "As I watched, thrones were set in place;

and the Ancient One took his seat.

His clothing was white as snow,

the hair on his head was like pure wool.

His throne was fiery flames,

with wheels of burning fire.

10 A stream of fire flowed from his presence;

thousands and thousands ministered to him,

millions and millions stood before him.

**Then the court was convened**, and the books were opened.

**11** "I kept watching. Then, because of the arrogant words

which the horn was speaking, **I watched as the animal was

killed; its body was destroyed**; and it was given over to be

burned up completely. **12** As for the other animals, **their

rulership was taken away;** but their lives were prolonged for

a time and a season."

Wouldn't it be great to know that when you pray for something; good things happen right away? And wouldn't it be great to know that you could be truly - I mean every single day truly - be on the winning side?

*Yes*

*prayer Make it happen immediately*

There was a time that I was hit and miss on all of my intercessory prayer attempts, and frankly, I was getting discouraged by the constant battle. **Discouraged**

It seemed that what I was doing was never enough and I felt the pressure to battle all the time. If you have ever been involved in intercessory prayer for any period of time you know what I'm talking about.

Like, when I would pray for my loved ones to be saved and come to Jesus. I would get my list out, begin to pray in the Spirit and scriptures, and try to feel like I was making headway. Regrettably I wasn't. For over 20 years.

Yup. No results for that long.

That's pretty discouraging huh? Maybe you can relate.

*Again...*
*Again*
*a-n*
*agai*

I would break the power of the enemy out of their lives - again. I would declare them free and their eyes opened - again. I would call their name before God - again. But it seemed my prayers were going nowhere.

Thankfully, Holy Spirit graciously opened my eyes to see there was a better way. He taught me about something in the heavenly realms that has radically changed my relationship with God for the better, and has increased my effectiveness in prayer dramatically and measurably. (BTW - our free 5 Day Salvation Challenge is where we teach you how to pray for your loved ones salvation.)

*Jesus' power*

Here's the deal, Jesus has all power and authority in heaven and on earth.

*All authority in heaven and Earth*

**Matt 28:18** (CJB)

Yeshua came and talked with them. He said, **"All authority in heaven and on earth has been given to me."**

It's a fact. Jesus has all authority not only in heaven but also on the earth. This is the restoration of the authority that God had given to Adam. In first Corinthians 15 Jesus is called the last Adam. When God created mankind on the earth he gave us - humanity - all the authority over everything.

But there was a slight problem that happened in the garden of Eden. Our first parents made a deal where they turned their authority over to someone we are calling the Adversary (satan, serpent, dragon), and he became our arch enemy.

It happened legally.

In order for Jesus to get the authority back into his control, it had to be done legally. We will talk about this in a few minutes.

Here's another instance where Jesus is recognized as having all authority and power.

**Revelation 5:6-14**

6 Then I saw standing there with the throne and the four living beings, in the circle of the elders, a Lamb that appeared to have been slaughtered. He had seven horns and seven eyes, which are the sevenfold Spirit of God sent out into all the earth. 7 He came and took the scroll out of the right hand of the One sitting on the throne. 8 When he took the scroll, the four living beings and the twenty-four elders fell down in front of the Lamb. Each one held a harp and

gold bowls filled with pieces of incense, which are the prayers
of God's people; **9** and they sang a new song,
"You are worthy to take the scroll and break its seals; because
you were slaughtered;
at the cost of blood you ransomed for God
persons from every tribe, language, people and nation.
10 You made them into a kingdom for God to rule,
*cohanim* to serve him;
and they will rule over the earth."
**11** Then I looked, and I heard the sound of a vast number
of angels — thousands and thousands, millions and millions!
They were all around the throne, the living beings and the
elders; **12** and they shouted out, "Worthy is the slaughtered
Lamb to receive power, riches, wisdom, strength, honor,
glory and praise!"
**13** And I heard every creature in heaven, on earth, under
the earth and on the sea — yes, everything in them —
saying,
"To the One sitting on the throne and to the Lamb
belong praise, honor, glory and power forever and ever!"
**14** The four living beings said, "*Amen!*" and the elders fell
down and worshipped."

In fact, if you keep reading in the passage at the beginning of this
chapter; Daniel 7, you'll see that Jesus's Kingdom is established over
all of the kingdoms of the earth.

**Daniel 7:13**

13 "I kept watching the night visions, when I saw, coming
with the clouds of heaven, someone like a son of man. He
approached the Ancient One and was led into his presence.
14 To him was given rulership, glory and a kingdom, so that
all peoples, nations and languages should serve him. His
rulership is an eternal rulership
that will not pass away; and his kingdom is one
that will never be destroyed."

He is the King of Kings and Lord of Lords. No one has more
power and authority than Jesus.

However, even though He has this power and authority, we still
see - on a daily basis - gross injustices happening to innocent and good
people all over the world. These injustices range from birth defects
and hereditary diseases to human trafficking victims, to abuses of all
kinds. Drug addictions, suicides, violence, war, theft, defamation,
division, betrayal, racism, famine, relational estrangement, trauma,
curses, and more. All of these seem to run rampant across the globe.

**This is a paradox that demands an answer as to WHY?**

**Why… if He has all power and authority, do these things still
happen on the earth?**

It's really quite simple. Adam and Eve sold their birthright to
the adversary and we're born again from spiritual life into spiritual
death. When that occurred everything they owned and had authority
over came into the possession of the adversary. From that day death
and destruction became possible on the earth especially in the lives of
human beings.

Satan's tactic was to use deception to get possession of Adam and Eve's authority. He hasn't changed how he operates. He still uses deception to get human beings to yield their authority to him. Anything that the adversary does in the lives of people and upon the earth is done through the use of human authority.

A human being, even without the spirit of God, has more authority than Satan, but without understanding what being born with DNA means on the earth, human beings continue to buy the lies that Satan tells them to yield their authority to him and for his use.

This is why in many cultures you see occult practices, witchcraft, polytheism, animism, blood oaths, curses - even celebrations of spring fertility like the MayDay Pole, these are all designed by the adversary to bring human beings into an agreement with him, or to renew an agreement with him.

If human beings stopped making these kinds of agreements, Satan would lose his grip on the earth in one day.

Every agreement made is in place legally. And as long as the agreements are in place Satan continues to use human power to bring death and destruction on the earth.

When a human being is born again into Jesus Christ, now the authority of Jesus is available to release the kingdom of heaven upon the earth. This is why healing and deliverance are the signs of the power of God. It is evidence that the Spirit of God is destroying the works of the devil.

When human beings yield their authority to Jesus Christ, God now has a gateway through which to establish his goodness on the earth. This is why we confess Jesus is Lord in order to be saved. That confession of the Lordship of Jesus causes your authority to be lent to Jesus Christ for the purposes of the kingdom of heaven.

*obey — long*
*faith — imp please*

# The Will of God is

The will of God is everlasting life. Where the kingdom of heaven is, everlasting life exists. This is why Jesus said that he has come that we might have life and have it more abundantly. (John 10:10) What Adam did brought death. Jesus brings life.

*Jesus partner*
*w/ those who trust him*

Though Jesus has all power and authority in heaven and on earth, he will only work in partnership with those that trust him. Because he himself shares in DNA, because he was born as a human being, because you trust in him, you now share in his everlasting life. And it is through your life that he establishes the kingdom of heaven on the earth in the hearts of the people that you come in contact with. It is the authority of Jesus working through a human being that brings life on the earth. This is how his kingdom is established upon the earth.

*kingdm est through your life*

Bad things will continue to happen to good people until those good people realize that they can get out of the agreement that they have made with the adversary, and make a new agreement with Jesus Christ. ✳

Jesus is Lord over all, and he works through those who fully trust in him. One of the adventures that we get to be on as children of God, is to establish the goodness of God in the land of the living. To demonstrate God's love, kindness, and goodness to all of mankind. ☆

**REVIEW OF CHAPTER 1:**

*Good people can stop bad things from happening when they are out of agreem w/ Adversary*

- Jesus has all power and authority under His control.
- Adam and Eve gave their authority to the adversary who then used it against them and against all of humanity.
- As long as human beings make deals with the devil, he will continue to reign in this world.
- When human beings yield their authority to Jesus by confessing Him as Lord, He is able to bring life into the earth through them.

*int to*

# CHAPTER 2:

# WHAT YOU DON'T SEE IS MORE REAL THAN WHAT YOU DO SEE

---

## HOW TO DO SPIRITUAL WARFARE THE RIGHT WAY

### BY GREG KURJATA

Jesus created both the visible and the invisible realms. Everything you can see and everything you cannot see, is created by Jesus. What you see with your physical eyes has function, and what you cannot see equally has function.

Just like there is a materiality to the physical world, there is a materiality to the invisible world as well. The physical world is made of matter, the heavenly realm is made of creative light - but it still has a materiality to it, meaning it has substance when you are in the heavenly realm.

*Pworld*
*vs*
*Heavenly realm*

### Colossians 1:15-17

**15** "He is the visible image of the invisible God. He is supreme over all creation, **16** because *in connection with him were created all things* — **in heaven and on earth, visible and invisible**, whether thrones, lordships, rulers or authorities — they have all been created through him and for him. **17** He existed before all things, and he holds everything together..."

We know the visible realm very well. We live in it via our 5 physical senses. We can see, hear, taste, touch and smell in this realm. Laws of physics govern the way that we function in this realm. We are trained to see, comprehend, act and react to the physical realm by simply living in this environment.

*Phy*

The invisible realm... not so much.

The only way to know about how to function in the invisible realm is the Bible. The word of God makes it possible for you to live in the invisible realm while still in the physical body. It teaches you how to see, how to hear, how to walk, and how to live in the invisible realm.

Jesus told us about the kingdom of heaven. He mentioned over and over again how the kingdom of heaven is at hand. What that means is the kingdom of heaven is within reach and it's easily accessible. Anybody can have access to it if they know how to get there. Jesus said you can enter the kingdom of heaven by being born again. If a person is born of the spirit, born from above, they will enter the kingdom of heaven. (John 3) He said if we humble ourselves like a little child we can enter the kingdom of heaven. (Matt 18)

So the kingdom of heaven is easily accessible if a child can do it.

The invisible realm is all around you. That's what being at hand means. It means it's within reach. In order for something to be within reach it needs to be close to you. This invisible realm is something that Jesus created for his purposes and his use.

It's a realm that you live in all the time and have varying degrees of consciousness of that realm.

You are a person of two realms. You are a Spirit made in the image and likeness of God (Gen 1:26-28) who is hosting a physical body (Gen 2:7). The Bible says that you are a citizen of heaven.

### Philippians 3:20-21

**20 "But we are citizens of heaven, and it is from there** that we expect a Deliverer, the Lord Yeshua the Messiah. **21** He will change the bodies we have in this humble state and make them like his glorious body, using the power which enables him to bring everything under his control."

Since you are a citizen of heaven, you are from there. You exist in the heavenly realm at the same time you exist in the physical realm.

Whichever realm you pay more attention to is the realm that you will function in more often.

*Which realm?!*

It becomes like a dimension shift.

One minute you're conscious of and aware of the physical realm, the next minute you're conscious of and in the heavenly realm. This is done by faith in the word of God.

Just like the physical realm exhibits the glory of God, in the same way the invisible realm is filled with the glory of God. In fact, the function of a scripture is to bring you into the reality of what that scripture is referring to in the kingdom of heaven. Scripture is a doorway, a pathway, a gateway, a window, into the heavenly realm.

The Bible also declares that you have been raised up to sit in heavenly places in Christ Jesus. (Eph 2, Col 3) You are in the same place that Jesus is in the heavenly realms. We'll talk about what being seated in the heavenly places means in a while.

Jesus by his spirit lives inside of your heart here on the earth, and you by your spirit live in Jesus in the heavenly places. Where he is you are, and where you are he is.

*WOW*

You cannot be separated from Jesus. You are a member of his body, of his flesh and bone (1 Cor 6:15). The Holy Spirit has already baptized you into the body of Jesus (1 Cor 12:13). You are one spirit with him (1 Cor 6:17).

*w/ Jesus*

Because all of this is true, you have way more power than you thought you did. You just need to know how that power functions in a legal way. Once you understand the legal process for the use of power, then everything will change for you.

You will understand how you will never feel powerless again.

*Have power — how it functions in a legal way.*

*(margin note: Pathways to Spiritual realm)*

## The Pathways Of The Word

The Scripture is filled with pathways that are designed to bring you into heavenly places. One of these pathways is Hebrews 4:16

16 "Therefore, **let us confidently approach the throne from which God gives grace,** so that we may receive mercy and find grace in our time of need."

Here's the question, where is this throne? Can you GPS it? Can you find it on Google maps? Do you need a passport to get there? Where is it on the earth?

*(margin note: Throne in heavenly places)*

It becomes obvious that you are being invited to approach a throne that does not exist in the physical realm. It only exists in the heavenly realm. The only way to get there is through the word of God, because this is the only way that you know this place exists.

It's also obvious in the scripture that you can approach the throne with confidence. So in order to get there you need confidence in Jesus, you need confidence that the place exists, and you need confidence that something good is going to happen when you get there.

The point is, it's in the invisible realm, and you already have the ability to go to this heavenly place that you can't see with your physical eyes. How do you get there? You get there through your trust in Jesus Christ and your trust in the word that he has spoken. When you act in line with what the word of God already says it will bring you into these heavenly realities.

*(margin note: wow)*

### 2 Corinthians 4:18 NIV

"So we **fix our eyes not on what is seen,** but **on what is unseen,** since what is seen is temporary, but **what is unseen is eternal.**"

*Fix eyes on unseen*

When the scripture says fix your eyes on what is unseen, it's not referring to your physical eyeballs. This is a mistake often made that we look at the form of something rather than the (function) of an item in scripture. So the question to ask is what is the function of an eye? It's in the function of an eye that the pathway to actually see eternal things is opened up.

The primary function of an eye is to capture enormous amounts of data and to ascribe understanding and meaning to that data. Of course this is a simplification. For example your ear hears in a range from 20 Hz to 20,000 Hz, but your eye sees in the range of 380 to 750 nanometers or 400 to 790 terahertz. The amount of data that your eye takes in is multiples times higher than what your ear takes in. Yet even with the amount of data that your physical eye can take in it is still limited to the physical realm.

*See in eternal realm by faith*

So how can we see into the eternal realm?

You do it by faith. 2 Corinthians 5:7 "...for we live **by trust** (or faith), not by **what we see**"

You trust that what the word of God tells you about, actually is. You allow the scriptures to give you access into the heavenly realm. You *TRUST* allow the logic of the heavenly realm to become normalized for your thinking. Your mind is renewed to the kingdom and biblical realities in this way. The unseen realm will become your normal realm - and it does not have to be weird or flaky. It works when you're shopping for groceries or watching Netflix.

There.

You just received an introductory crash course in becoming a mature son or daughter of God.

*Allow Scriptures to give you access to Ht. realm. normalized for your thinking*

A mature son or daughter of God is a believer in Jesus who is grown up in their understanding of how things function in the invisible world. They walk in power. They walk in humility. They walk in love. These are the ones with whom God reveals the secrets of his covenant.

This is one of the areas that we have specialized in regarding helping people to get to that place of breakthrough in their heart in their mind to where they are confident in their spirit regarding who they are in Christ. Having someone to mentor you in this area would be of great value to you.

For that reason we have created resources and a community that is available to serve you in this great quest. It requires an investment of time, energy and money, but will yield a tremendous return in your life. Check out **The God First Process** for more details: **www.GodFirstProcess.com** This is the shortest path I know of to a happier and richly powerful spiritual life.

Next!

# CHAPTER 3:

# HOW THE FORCES OF DARKNESS GET THEIR POWER

———

HOW TO DO SPIRITUAL WARFARE THE RIGHT WAY

BY GREG KURJATA

So far we have looked at the kingdom of heaven, and how you have access to the invisible realm through the word of God. *Access through scripture*

As a son or daughter of God, you have at your disposal all the power and authority of Jesus Christ because of the Holy Spirit and His Name. He has all power all authority in heaven and on earth. When you know how to function in his name, that same power is available to you.

But you need to do it legally.

There are two sides to the spiritual world that surrounds you. On the good side is the kingdom of heaven that Jesus said is at hand - anything good and beneficial to humanity is within that realm. On the bad side; are organized and evil intentioned forces and beings. They have been entrenched for thousands of years, and know a whole lot more about how things operate on earth and in the invisible spirit world than the average person. Meaning, they know how to use human authority better than human beings do.

The spiritual structure that these disembodied spirits occupy had originally been created for, and given to, Adam and Eve. It is represented by things like thrones, mountains and hills.

For example when Satan was tempting Jesus in Luke chapter 4, he took him to the peak of a very high mountain and showed him all the kingdoms of the world. He was not standing on Mount Everest or any earthly mountain. He was standing in this spiritual structure within which all of the kingdoms of the world were visible.

He told Jesus, "all of this has been given to me, and I can give it to whomever I wish." *Lie*

Where did Satan get all of the kingdoms of the world? He got them from Adam, and was **using Adam's power** to bring destruction into the creation of God.

*The Fall*

Genesis 3 tells about the event that caused the transfer of the title ownership of this entire spiritual structure. It was meant to produce only life, peace, love, hope, blessing, health, success, with good and beneficial things. But once the adversary took possession, it began to produce only wickedness, death, hate, greed, depression, sorrow, pain, deception - and so much more.

The adversary had gained control of the power through Adam and Eve coming into an agreement with him. This legal contract has been the basis of all the death and destruction that you see in the lives of people on the earth. In fact the only real power that the adversary has now is power given to him by a human being. The big difference is he knows exactly how to use that authority to bring oppression into that persons life.

*Break ties w/Adv.*

## JESUS ESTABLISHED JUSTICE ON THE EARTH, AND WHY THIS MATTERS TO YOU

*Legally, Jesus Got it all back*

Jesus's death, burial, resurrection and ascension into heaven began the process of getting that structure back into the hands of humanity. He acted for all of us - the legal term is class action.

*No. choice*

The effect of what Jesus did is this; justice has been established upon the earth. We had nothing to do with the decision that Adam and Eve made, yet we all were born into the chaos of their decision. It isn't right nor fair that we were born into sin, death, sickness, darkness, poverty, heartache etc. We had nothing to do with their decision, yet we suffer the consequences of their decision.

*We Need Justice*

The only solution to this problem is justice.

This is why Jesus died on the cross, to establish justice on the earth and make it right with humanity for what Adam and Eve had done. God made it right with you regarding the decision Adam and Eve had made. You had nothing to do with their decision, and you had nothing to do with God's decision to save you by sending Jesus, other than being someone He loves.

Jesus made it right so that we could have our authority, our power, our position, our life restored to what God had originally intended. The entire kingdom of Adam is now **legally** under the control of Jesus, but the eviction of the previous tenants - the forces of darkness - has not yet been completed.

This is one of the great purposes of prayer, specifically praying in the Courts Of Heaven.

As long as people continue to make agreements, deals, oaths, and covenants with the adversary, in whatever form that happens, the kingdom of darkness will continue to operate.

Like I mentioned earlier, if people quit doing this - things would be dramatically different on the earth. The evil spirits would have no legal rights to remain active, and their footholds would be destroyed.

This is because they have no actual authority of their own. They use derived authority to do what they do. Meaning that they deceive people into lending them their authority to take footholds and beachheads in societies and cultures. Just like satan did with Adam and Eve.

This is why the bible warns against all forms of idolatry, witchcraft, satanic rituals, necromancy, fortune telling, along with any and all demonically inspired teachings, secret societies, and religions - these are the traps and snares evil spirits use to get people to lend their authority to them.

God isn't an egotistical jerk who demands all the attention when he gave the commandment to have no other gods besides him. Rather, He knows how powerful human authority is on the earth. He knows

*Protection*

how it works, and He has been trying to protect people from turning their lives over to something so base and dark.

Whenever people turn to God with all of their hearts, a wellspring of life is opened up within them, and good begins to happen for them because of getting back to their original created purpose.

To win at spiritual warfare - you must learn to operate in the spiritual realms **legally**.

The bible is the only book that deals with this realm with authority. In Ephesians 6, Paul, one of the Apostles, wrote this instruction to the saints in Ephesus:

### Ephesians 6:10-12

*God speaks to what we fight against*

**10** "Finally, grow powerful in union with the Lord, in union with his mighty strength! **11** Use all the armour and weaponry that God provides, so that you will be able to stand against the deceptive tactics of the Adversary. **12** For we are not struggling against human beings, but against the rulers, authorities and cosmic powers governing this darkness, against the spiritual forces of evil in the heavenly realm."

He points out that our true struggle is against an organized evil and spiritual structure, not against other people. He mentions how deception is a tactic utilized by this group, and then itemized who they are. Here's the list:

1. rulers
2. authorities
3. cosmic powers governing darkness
4. spiritual forces of evil in the heavenly realm.

*Organized use distraction to divide* (handwritten annotation)

So, how much do we actually know about these guys and their function? Sadly, very little. However, we can see that they are active and working on the earth in every form of evil and darkness that manifests.

These beings are called evil spirits and demons. In Jesus' ministry, He spent quite some time casting out evil spirits from people - and in some cases, these evil entities were the direct cause of the sickness or mental problems a person was having. (I don't have time to go through all of those events in the gospels, but if you read through Matthew, Mark, Luke, and John, you'll find them.)

*Jesus dealt w. evil demons* (handwritten annotation)

They are obviously organized having rulers and authorities, and governance over darkness. They have a goal of some kind and they know how to distract and divide their enemy - which is all of mankind.

A question you should be asking is why did Satan go after Adam and Eve and take things over?

**The answer is he wanted access to DNA.**

Without DNA he could not have any authority on the earth, or over anything that God created visible and invisible. God gave all creation to a being made in his image who possessed DNA.

Angels do not reproduce. Heavenly beings do not reproduce. Human beings reproduce. When God created the universe he gave it to a man and a woman to have and exercise authority over everything he created. Beings with DNA now had dominion over the created universe both visible and invisible.

Satan wanted the dominion and the only way he could get it was by a covenant with the ones who had the dominion. So he deceived them into an agreement but did not disclose all of the terms and conditions connected to that agreement.

*How Satan got Control* (handwritten annotation)

He did not disclose that as soon as they agreed with him that their light would go out, that they would die physically, that their children would die, that they would be spiritually blind. Also that they would be kicked out of Eden, lose control of the invisible realm that Jesus had created for them, and would be left destitute trying to survive on cursed ground.

The next stage of his plan was to try to reproduce his own DNA. The origin of evil spirits goes back to the time of Noah. In that time prior to the flood, the Bible (Gen 6) talks about how a small company of angels left their place of authority to overshadow women and have children by those women. The Bible mentions these children were giants.

There are various writings from those times which outline what happened and the outcome that has affected us to this day. One of those writings is the book of Enoch. The Book of Enoch is quoted numerous times in the New Testament (eg. Jude 1:14-15, 2 Peter 2:4). Within the book of Enoch is a conversation between God and Enoch. In that conversation God is pronouncing judgement upon these creatures that were born of women, but were not of his creation.

### Book of Enoch, Section 1 Chapter 15:8-12

[8] And now, the giants, who are produced from the spirits and flesh, shall be called evil spirits upon [9] the earth, and on the earth shall be their dwelling. Evil spirits have proceeded from their bodies; because they are born from men and from the holy Watchers is their beginning and primal origin; [10] they shall be evil spirits on earth, and evil spirits shall they be called. [As for the spirits of heaven, in heaven shall be their dwelling, but as for the spirits of the earth which were born upon the

earth, on the earth shall be their dwelling.] **And the spirits of the giants afflict, oppress, destroy, attack, do battle, and work destruction on the earth, and cause trouble: they take no food, but nevertheless [12] hunger and thirst, and cause offences.** And these spirits shall rise up against the children of men and against the women, because they have proceeded from them.

A good resource that does a good job of explaining the Book of Enoch is The Lost Prophet - The Book Of Enoch and it's Influence on Christianity by Margaret Barker (Click the linked title above to see it on Amazon.)

These are the beings that had taken over the kingdom of Adam. In Colossians 1 it mentions how Jesus created the visible and the invisible realm including thrones, dominions, rulers, and authorities all things were created by Him and for his use. This indicates a spiritual structure that was to be occupied by righteous men and women. After what Adam and Eve did, that spiritual structure became occupied by these evil spirits.

Their entire focus has been to get people into agreements with them so they can manifest on the earth. They need connection to the ground, and especially connection with DNA. Since they don't have any of their own authority, they do the same thing Satan did to Adam and Eve; they deceive people into giving them their human authority.

To summarize, Jesus has all power and authority since his resurrection from the dead and ascension into heaven. However, the adversary still occupies the invisible realm that had been created by Jesus for his use, via agreements that human beings continue to make with him. These agreements have legal force and effect in the invisible realm and remain in place until they are challenged legally in the court system of heaven.

# CHAPTER 4:
# MY BACK STORY

In order to understand my discovery, you'll need some of my backstory for it to make some sense to you.

I received Jesus as my Lord and saviour when I was 20 years old. It was August 6, 1982, and it was 9 PM on a Friday night.

I was watching television in my brothers living room when suddenly I heard a voice that said, "Greg, get up and get into your truck and drive."

For obvious reasons I was concerned.

I was hearing a voice who knew my name and was telling me to do something. My first thought was maybe I had done too many drugs and I was now hearing voices.

Again the voice spoke, "Get up, get your keys, get into your truck, and drive."

I felt compelled to obey what this voice was telling me to do. So I got my keys, got in my truck, backed out of my brothers driveway, started driving, came to a stop sign and turned left.

When I was half way down the hill from the stop sign something happened.

In the snap of a finger, I was pulling into a parking lot that was across the street from a Christian coffeehouse which was one and a half kilometres away from where the hill was.

I had been translocated. My truck, everything in my truck, and me - were translocated one and a half kilometres.

I was freaked out. I had no idea how I had arrived at the parking lot.

Suddenly, the voice that had been in my brothers living room was now in my truck. It said, "Go inside, sit down and listen."

The coffeehouse was operated by a group of Christian young people and was hosted by the local Anglican Church. I found out two weeks later that they had been praying prior to the meeting start time and asking God to send his angels to bring people to the meeting that needed to be there. At the exact moment of their prayers is when the voice spoke to me.

I went inside. sat down and listened, and everything that was said and done that evening inspired me and caused me to think that perhaps God is closer than I thought He was. I felt I could make a connection with him that night.

At about 11 PM on the sidewalk outside of the coffeehouse I bowed my head and prayed that Jesus would become my Lord and my Saviour. My life was transformed from that night. Ever since then I have been walking with Jesus.

I was baptized in the Holy Spirit about a month later and spoke with tongues. Then 2 months after that, I was baptized in water. That is when my spiritual life accelerated. It was like someone poured gasoline over me and lit a match. I was on fire for Jesus.

I could not get enough of the bible.

I spent 8 to 18 hours a day studying, praying, listening to teaching, and talking about the things of God. It was a joyful and wonderful time of discovery. I became a bonafide card-carrying bibleaholic and Word Nerd. I love the Word of God and live by it as best as I know how.

It was so exciting. Everyday was a new discovery of truth. Everyday was a new experience of the love and goodness of God. Everyday was also a struggle against some unseen forces that I could feel pushing against me to try and keep me from growing in the knowledge of Jesus.

I was aware of the realm of darkness because of being involved in occult activity when I was a teenager. I knew there were evil spirits already as I had encountered them before I was a follower of Jesus. What I didn't know was how to deal with that stuff, so I bought some books and read them, and listened to some teaching on the authority of the Name of Jesus and spiritual warfare.

I won't go into everything I had learned in that time, but some of it was pretty good. It showed me that I, as a son of God had the right to use the Name of Jesus to heal the sick, cast out devils and preach the gospel of Jesus with power. (Mark 16:17-20, John 14:12, Matt 10:7-8, Acts 3:16) That His Name was all powerful and that evil spirits would have to respond to the name of Jesus. (Luke 10:18-19, Matt 28:18) I experienced this in action many times.

I discovered I could have a personal friendship with the Holy Spirit, because when you see Holy Spirit you see Jesus. His job is to reveal everything Jesus has given to us. (see John 16:7-15 and 1 Corinthians 2:10-12)

Angels/partners

I also learned about angels and how they are partners in the kingdom together with people to bring about the kingdom of God on the earth. (Heb 1:14, Ps 91, Ps 103:19-22) How there are many classes of angels and each class has a different function that ranges from worship to warfare.

Worship to Warfare Jobs

Then there was the part about the authority of mankind, in that God would not do anything on the earth unless he did it in agreement with a person on the earth.

The contrast with what I said earlier about the kingdom of darkness not having any of their own authority and using derived authority vs what God does is this: God has actual authority over all things and is the Author and Creator of all things. However, He has already delegated the rulership of the universe to mankind and He won't take it back. So by His choice He partners with people to accomplish what is best for humanity. He will always act through the trust and actions of people.

WOW

This is called trust or faith. Hebrews 11:6 says:

> And without **trusting**, it is impossible to be **well pleasing to God**, because whoever approaches him must **trust** that he does exist and that he becomes a Rewarder to those who seek him out.

Everything that God does He does in response to faith or trust. Trust is something that originates in Him, (Rom 10:17) and as He trusts us, we learn to trust Him, ourselves and others.

These were some of the keys of what I learned. All of them are good and work extremely well.

But, some of my experience was different.

At times, I struggled with sin in my life, and when I tried to help some people with certain kinds of problems - like demon possession, curses, or poltergeist activity, I couldn't help them at all. Even though I was using the name of Jesus, trusting God, and cooperating with the Holy Spirit to the best of my ability, nothing would happen.

At the same time I was seeing miracles - real ones - of biblical proportions - but I knew there was more to learn that would help me to be more effective.

I had a policy when it came to the word of God. This policy was if I found something that I could act upon in the Bible that I would do it. I wasn't always successful at it but I tried my best. I would try to take action on something new every day and as a result I saw the power of God begin to move in my life.

But when it came to spiritual warfare I was often flying blind. I didn't know what I was doing. I was just trying to do something that someone said in a book or on a tape.

We MUST TRUST
God. period.

— Pleases God

God Rewards those
who seek Him.

← Real
   prayer / Struggle

← Biblical

# CHAPTER 5:

# HOW I LEARNED SPIRITUAL WARFARE THE WRONG WAY

---

## HOW TO DO SPIRITUAL WARFARE THE RIGHT WAY

### BY GREG KURJATA

A few years into my walk with Jesus, I got in with a group of folks who believed in intercession and spiritual warfare. This is when I learned spiritual warfare tactics that were wrong, and regrettably, the majority of folks into intercession and spiritual warfare today still read the same books and follow the same path.

We would pray for hours, and in that time I would "see and hear" many things in the "spirit" that confused me.

For instance, I would begin to pray against what I perceived as an evil spirit influence on an issue or situation, and as I prayed I would "hear" in my thoughts things like, "You can't do that. You don't have the authority to do that!" To which I would quote a long list of scriptures to "fight with" by saying - like Jesus - "It is written..." (Matthew and Luke 4). I figured that since Jesus fought the devil in this way that I could do the same thing. By saying it is written then quoting scripture I thought that was like shooting a gun at the devil.

Also for some reason I thought the can of spiritual "whoop-ass" I was serving up should be done hot and loud - so I would often be yelling these things.

Sometimes something would happen, and it would encourage me to keep using this tactic, but more often, nothing would happen. I never knew about the spiritual legal system that's in place so I had no idea about the legal agreements in the spiritual realm.

So hearing in the spirit that I didn't have a right to do something I saw Jesus doing in the word was confusing to me. The way I reasoned with it was I thought the devil is a liar so why should I believe what he saying? But the reality is because of my ignorance I was hurting myself.

I knew the bible said that I had all authority over the power of the enemy...

## Luke 10:17-19

**17** The seventy came back jubilant. "Lord," they said, "with your power, even the demons submit to us!" **18** Yeshua said to them, "I saw Satan fall like lightning from heaven. **19** Remember, I have given you authority; so you can trample down snakes and scorpions, indeed, all the Enemy's forces; and you will remain completely unharmed. **20** Nevertheless, don't be glad that the spirits submit to you; be glad that your names have been recorded in heaven."

...but I couldn't seem to get this passage working for me like I knew it could work.

Around that time I would bind the devil every day, and I would rebuke him many times a day. I remember asking myself one day, "If I'm binding the devil everyday - when is he bound? If I am rebuking the devil everyday - when is he rebuked? Why do I feel the need to continue doing this every-single-day?"

Sadly the answer to that question didn't arrive for a couple of years. Not completely sure why, but it didn't stop me from following that same pattern of spiritual warfare. Honestly, I didn't know any better.

Then other groups started to do spiritual mapping and digging into the historical backgrounds of areas in the hope of finding what the ruling spirit over an area might be, so that warfare could be waged against that thing. It seemed that they knew way more about what the devil was doing than what God was doing.

Then I would notice that whenever this kind of warfare was conducted, there would be a terrible backlash and all hell would break loose in a prayer group or church. It was serious stuff too! People got sick, people died, marriages and ministries were destroyed - I could

Backlash

go on. **Again, I was confused. If we have all authority in the name of Jesus - how could stuff like this happen?**

It was almost a badge of honour to have backlash.

People would say, and maybe you have said this yourself, "I must really be doing something right - look at all this proverbial "crap hitting the fan" in my life right now. Devil must be mad!"

You're not doing something right - you're doing something wrong - and that's exactly why you have that kind of chaos going on in your life.

During this season of my life I read books on prayer and intercession, I attended conferences on spiritual warfare, I wrote songs and led congregations in spiritual warfare prayers and songs. I followed the processes of the teachers of the day, and tried to innovate some of my own ideas.

Again, there were times it worked, but more often than not, it caused grief and sorrow. And I was doing it to myself without knowing what was going on.

Maybe you're nodding your head in agreement. Perhaps you've done the exact same thing. Perhaps you've been as confused as I was when I tried to get free from what I perceived as evil spirits, or to drive them off situations when I encountered them.

It wasn't until I encountered the courts of heaven that I got the answers I needed to function in line with the way things actually are. The Holy Spirit taught me about the legal system that governs the invisible realms.

Ignorance is very expensive.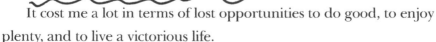

It cost me a lot in terms of lost opportunities to do good, to enjoy plenty, and to live a victorious life.

We can help you to navigate this area of your life within our community. Our focus is to create an environment of growth and transformation through experience of the Word of God in the heavenly realms. We have weekly broadcasts on our Facebook and YouTube Channels on Thursdays and Sundays, along with resources like our online video course called **Justice and the Courts of Heaven**, that will show you how to legally function fully in the heavenly realm. Go to https://www.jchonline.ca/jchcourse

Justice and the
Courts of Heaven

# CHAPTER 6:
# HOW TO DO SPIRITUAL WARFARE THE RIGHT WAY

———

HOW TO DO SPIRITUAL WARFARE THE RIGHT WAY

BY GREG KURJATA

In 2006, I was in the custom of doing a certain style of spiritual warfare prayer I call the Carlos Anacondia Prayer.

Carlos is a famous Argentinian Evangelist that stepped out in faith and brought revival to his country. His signature prayer was this one: "Now, you listen to me satan..." and then he would proceed to break the power of the devil and have great results. Demons would begin screaming out, sicknesses would get healed, lost souls would be saved.

He got great results around the world utilizing this prayer. I thought, "If it worked for him it should work for me too!" And so, when I would pray, at some point in my praying time, I would go into that mode of prayer.

One August night, on a lake, I began to pray that way again. No sooner had I said, "Now, you listen to me satan..." when the Holy Spirit stood in front of me and said,

"You know Greg, He's been at this a lot longer than you have. You need some help."

Instantly I found myself in a heavenly place, like an open vision - but not a vision - it seemed way too real to be a vision. In that place I saw a throne, and someone on the throne was hearing cases of people who were before the throne. Each one was given a scroll which they took back into their lives and I could see the effect of that ruling in their lives - like a video sequence in a movie.

I got excited and stepped in front of the throne myself to ask for justice for something that had happened to me 20 years earlier. It was related to ministry and church around which I felt a grave injustice was done against me.

As I made my petition, I was given a ruling in the form of a scroll. Then, just like I saw the others take the scroll back into their lives, I did the same thing and suddenly was back in the prayer room I was in.

Wow, what an effect that ruling had.

My entire heart felt relief and satisfaction that what I had suffered was being properly dealt with.

I felt vindicated.

I felt like justice had been done on my behalf.

The feeling of injustice that had surrounded me for 20 years was now gone and it happened instantly.

My next thought was to go back for more.

So, as I began the process of returning, the Holy Spirit stopped me by warning me in this way,

"Stop! You don't know what you are doing and are about to get into a lot of trouble. Let me take your case!"

The fear of God filled my heart in that moment and I was more than willing to let Him proceed.

I won't get into all of the details of what he told me, and how what happened changed my life as a result of that first court session, but you can see the video of my testimony about this on our YouTube channel - www.youtube.com/courtsofheaven. It's part of our online video course that I just mentioned.

That first encounter with the Courts Of Heaven was so dramatic in terms of real and authentic change in my life, that I felt compelled to learn everything I could about it. During the next seven years I researched the scriptures, experimented with discoveries in the Word of God, and learned all about justice from a heavenly perspective.

No one else was talking about the Courts Of Heaven around that time, or at least I was not in their orbit if there was anyone talking about it. So I never read anyone else's books or watched anyone's videos about the Courts Of Heaven.

Frankly, I was shocked to find the theme of justice and a court system all over the bible starting in Genesis 3 all the way to Revelation 20. It was like finding a treasure hidden in plain sight.

Then in 2013, we - my wife and I, began to teach publicly what we had learned privately over those seven years.

## THE INITIAL LESSONS ON THE COURTS OF HEAVEN

One day I was studying Daniel 7 and the Holy Spirit began to teach me about the power of the court in relation to spiritual warfare.

**Here's Daniel 7:9-11 again:**

9 "As I watched, **thrones were set in place**;

and the **Ancient One took his seat**.

His clothing was white as snow,

the hair on his head was like pure wool.

**His throne was fiery flames**,

with wheels of burning fire.

10 A stream of fire flowed from his presence;

thousands and thousands ministered to him,

millions and millions stood before him.

**Then the court was convened, and the books were opened.**

11 "I kept watching. Then, because of the arrogant words

which the horn was speaking, I watched **as the animal was**

**killed; its body was destroyed; and it was given over to be**

**burned up completely. 12 As for the other animals, their**

**rulership was taken away;** but their lives were prolonged for

a time and a season.

I absolutely love this passage of scripture. It reveals a heavenly realm that still exists and is functioning as much today as it was in the days of Daniel.

Let's break it down.

Daniel starts describing this by saying **thrones** - plural - were set in place. (*I discovered that anywhere the bible mentions a throne, there is a court in session. In the new testament the most notable ones are Hebrews 4:16 and Revelation 4. Both of these indicate a judicial action being present with the throne.*) This means the thrones were not in this place prior to them being SET in place. This indicates that it is a mobile court of some kind, and there was more than one magistrate in attendance of the court proceedings.

In ancient times, the elders and judges of a community would set their "seats" or thrones in the city gates, and in that place they would deal with community business and the settling of disputes among the people. In the book of Job chapter 29, Job mentions how he would set his seat in the city gate and then function as a judge among the people.

The thrones are now set in place, and the Ancient One takes HIS SEAT. I love the poetic imagery of this - the Ancient One. Another translation uses Ancient of Days to describe Him. This is none other than the Lord Almighty, the King of the Universe.

Daniel then describes what He looked like: Clothing white as snow, and hair white like wool, speaks of purity and without guile. Pure holiness and justice. Then the throne gets its own description of being on fire - even having wheels, which supports the idea of the throne being mobile.

Then this - a stream of FIRE flowing from His Presence. This is the glory of the Ancient One that creatively purifies all that it touches.

It's also functions as the fiery judgment of God against His enemies, with the same fire bringing blessing and favour to His saints.

The Ancient One was not alone as thousands and thousands ministered to Him - meaning they were agents of the court at the ready to assist and carry out the actions of the court. These are angels that participate in the execution of the judgements of the courts when they are executed upon the earth.

Then finally, millions upon millions were in attendance. These are the witnesses, or could be the people who were under the oppression of the unseen realm, and God was going to free them.

Then the pièce de résistance: **Then the court was convened, and the books were opened.** All of the pomp up to this point was for this reason - court needed to go into session.

The books mentioned are most likely the Book of Life - related to each person in the court, perhaps the Book of National Purposes - related to the evil empire entities and everything they had said and done that they needed to be held accountable for, and perhaps the Book of the Purposes of God for the nations. Whatever these books were, they were the basis of the judgement that was about to be released through this court.

What happened next in this passage was what the Holy Spirit used to teach me about how to conduct spiritual warfare. Remember, my first encounter with the Court of Heaven was because He told me I needed help to be effective in spiritual warfare.

Here it is:

**11** "I kept watching. Then, because of the arrogant words which the horn was speaking, I watched **as the animal was killed**; its **body was destroyed;** and it was **given over to be burned up completely.**

**12** As for the other animals, **their rulership was taken away**; but their lives were prolonged for a time and a season.

To recap, here's the sequence of events.

1. Thrones are set in place
5. The Ancient One takes His seat and releases Glory as fire
6. Everyone involved shows up
7. The court goes into session and books are opened
8. The court judges the evil empires and they are destroyed in the judgements. Check out the bolded sections of verse 11.

Nothing happened **UNTIL THE COURT WENT INTO SESSION.** Once the court went into session and the ruling was given, then the enemy was defeated RIGHT AWAY!

Immediately.

Pronto.

Instantaneously.

Now!

Now

There was no wailing and yelling at the devil to make him comply, just a court ruling that made it impossible for him to do anything **BUT** comply with the ruling. Notice, there was no backlash to Daniel regarding the vision, though it did alarm him somewhat - which most real heavenly encounters will do to you.

Two more times in Daniel 7 it refers to the court ruling in the favour of His people:

> **21** "I watched, and that horn made war with the holy ones and was winning, **22 until the Ancient One came, judgment was given in favour of the holy ones of the Most High**, and the time came for the holy ones to take over the kingdom."

and

**26** "But **when the court goes into session,** he will be **stripped of his rulership,** which will be consumed and completely destroyed."

It takes the court going into session to effectively deal with the evil in the spiritual realm. This was the lesson from the Holy Spirit to me, and my introduction to the Courts of Heaven.

# CHAPTER 7:

# HOW SPIRITUAL WARFARE TAKES PLACE

---

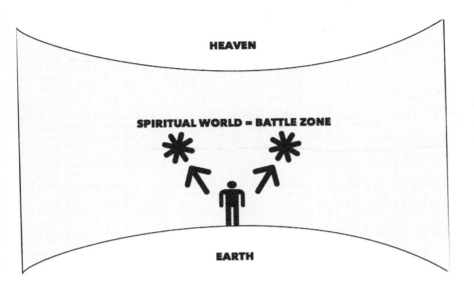

Here's a picture to help illustrate how warfare has been commonly, and incorrectly practised, and then one about how it should be done:

We've been taught to engage the enemy in spiritual battle by attacking from a position on the earth and sort of "praying up into" the place that has been called the 2nd heaven. *(it really isn't a second heaven but people call it that. I talk about what it actually is in one of the sessions of our course).* The warfare prayers consisted of scriptures, "binding and loosing," declaring, prophesying etc - all of it directed into that spiritual world battle zone where the evil darkness is set up.

Like in Ephesians 6:11-12. It says

11 Use all the armour and weaponry that God provides, so that you will be able to stand against the deceptive tactics of the Adversary. 12 For we are not struggling against human

beings, but against the rulers, authorities and cosmic powers governing this darkness, against the spiritual forces of evil in the heavenly realm."

*Spiritual realm*

These rulers, authorities, cosmic powers governing this darkness, and spiritual forces of evil are in the heavenly realm. This is the realm that surrounds the earth within which the kingdom of Adam was structured. Somehow these evil entities are organized and function. But we can't see them with our physical eyes. So we do the best we can by making assumptions about how they function.

I'm over simplifying, but if you have ever done spiritual warfare you do understand. And don't get me wrong, there is a real enemy of mankind that exists and it needs to be resisted, but this is not the way to do it.

Here's what I learned from the Holy Spirit about how to do battle in the spiritual world based on Daniel 7:

This is the way to do it.

**HEAVENLY COURT**

**SPIRITUAL WORLD = BATTLE ZONE**

**EARTH**

Look at this verse from Isaiah 54:17 (CJB)

> "No weapon made will prevail against you.
> ***In court you will refute every accusation.***
> The servants of *Adonai* inherit all this;
> the reward for their righteousness is from me,"

## ACCUSATIONS AND DEFENCE HAPPEN IN COURT

I underlined and bolded the line I wanted you to see. In court you will refute every accusation. The enemy uses legal proceedings in the heavenly realms to bring accusations against the saints, day and night, before God. Check out Revelation 12:10...

> "Then I heard a loud voice in heaven saying,
> "Now have come God's victory, power and kingship,
> and the authority of his Messiah;
> ***because the Accuser of our brothers,***
> ***who accuses them day and night before God,***
> ***has been thrown out!""***

According to this verse accusations could be getting registered against you day and night, however Isa 54:17 says that you are to deal with those accusations in court as part of the "no weapon formed against you" prospering.

Look at 1 Peter 5:8

> 8 "Stay sober, stay alert! Your **enemy, the Adversary**, stalks about like a roaring lion looking for someone to devour."

In the footnotes of The Passion Translation, the author gives this insight into the word ENEMY/ADVERSARY used in the verse:

"The Greek word antidikos is a legal term for one who presses a lawsuit that **must be defended**."

The Greek Lexicon states this meaning:

an opponent in a **suit of law**

*Important*

You could have accusations - lawsuits - happening against you in a heavenly court system at this very minute - but do you know how to defend yourself?

And what if you don't show up to court?

What do you think the judge will do?

Do you even know?

Do you know where the court is that you need to go to?

Do you know how to get there?

Do you realize how important this information is to you and your family?

The reality is the majority of people alive today do not know this place even exists let alone go there and do something! The enemy relies on your ignorance of what is legally available to you to defeat you. You need to know about this. You need **to know the scriptures** and **how to get there**, and **what to do** when you get there.

When your enemy the "*adversary - antidikos*" attacks - you must defend yourself, but the defending happens in a heavenly court. It's the only way to deal with the "devouring" of the "roaring lion" of the adversary. You need a ruling in your favour from the court of heaven, just like it is mentioned in Daniel 7:21-22 and Luke 18:1-10.

*You need a ruling in*

## THE WIDOW AND THE UNJUST JUDGE

Luke 18:1-10 Jesus used a story of a judge and a widow woman to illustrate a way to win battles legally to deal with oppression.

*Jesus Example*

The story goes like this (my paraphrase).

The widow woman had a man trying to ruin her life. This man was making her life miserable, most likely by trying to steal her property and inheritance left by her deceased husband. Even though that property was legally hers, it didn't stop this man from trying to take it.

Her action in the court was what saved her. She went before this judge to get a ruling to stop the man who was trying to ruin her. She knew that a ruling, or judgment, from the judge would end the actions of that man, because of the power within a judgment from the court.

The judge in this story was ungodly. But that didn't matter. When he gave this woman a ruling in her favour, it ended her suffering and dealt harshly with the man trying to ruin her. With the ruling of the court in her favour, she now had the full force of the government to support her.

Then Jesus said this:

*Wow!*

### Luke 18:7-8

7 Now won't God grant justice to his chosen people who cry out to him day and night? Is he delaying long over them? 8 I tell you that he will judge in their favour, and quickly! But when the Son of Man comes, will he find this trust on the earth at all?"

*God will rule in Our favor Quickly*

This statement implies that we can continually petition God for justice. He is willing to provide justice, and He wants to rule in our favour to rid our lives, and the lives of those around us of injustices. In addition, it appears that the trust that the Son of Man will be looking for is trust in the justice of God.

*Your favor*  *Yes! Justice*

*God's Justice*

*win*

## WIN THE BATTLE LEGALLY

The point is this: The battle is won legally.

The battle **IS** a legal battle.

*Spiritual Warfare & Backlash*

When you do spiritual warfare via the courts of heaven, you win every time - with zero backlash.

*Backlash*

This is why we created the online course Justice and the Courts of Heaven: To help good people to be better at what they feel passionate about, winning battles to set people free. If you want more info you can get it at: www.jchonline.ca.

*Intercessory Prayer*

I've been in prayer meetings where people are swinging swords, blowing shofars, waving flags, binding/loosing, declaring, screaming etc, and have done some of that myself, but the net effect was - not much happened. And backlash.

We could NOT quantify and say with confidence that what we did in that prayer meeting had any measurable effect on anything that we were dealing with by praying that way. It's frustrating and frankly, depressing. This is one of the reasons a lot of intercessors struggle with depression.

So in order to be effective in spiritual warfare you need to know about and access the heavenly courts to obtain the rulings and judgements of that court, and then use those judgements to fight against the enemy in the spiritual world.

## THE COURTS OF HEAVEN PRODUCE REAL RESULTS

Does it work?

A Big Yes!

### Little Boy Healed Of Autism

One of our students obtained justice through the courts of heaven for a little boy who had been abused and was severely autistic. After she prayed the boy was instantly and miraculously healed - his doctor verified it.

### Drug Dealers Busted By Police

On a local level, there had been a drug overdose in a part of my city, and for some reason it really affected me. I went into the court of heaven for justice for the family of this girl, for the community and for our city, and asked God to judge the dealers and manufacturers of the drugs. Within 2 weeks, the police announced they had dismantled an entire drug ring that was connected to that girl's death and 68 people were arrested.

### Unpaid Debt Paid The Next Day

A friend had sublet his apartment while he was working elsewhere. The problem happened when the renter did not pay the rent for a few months, then disappeared. My friend texted me one day with how frustrated he was with the situation. He was a student of our course so I reminded him about going to the heavenly court to deal with it there. The next day the renter called him and told him he would repay the money the day after!

### National Law Changed

On a national level, one of our live classes went into the courts of heaven on behalf of the judges of our nation and on behalf of children across our nation. We collectively asked for rulings related to family justice, safety for children, etc. Within a week, the chief justice of the Supreme Court put a committee together to revamp family law - to move it from an adversarial to a mediation approach. The article was on the front page of a national newspaper. It became law 5 years later.

## THOUSANDS GIVE THEIR LIVES TO JESUS

In the past season we have seen thousands of people come to Jesus via our 5 Day Salvation Challenge (jchonline.ca/5dsc) During the 5 days we train the challengers to make their own petition in the Courts of Heaven for their lost loved ones. What we have found is when they understand how to defeat the adversary legally, the lights come on. One lady prayed for her neighbour the FIRST day of the challenge in which I taught about Blinded Minds. The next day he came upstairs and asked to be saved.

THE NEXT DAY! Praise God, Praise God, Praise God.

We have testimonies of court cases being resolved, money owed - paid right away, family conflicts resolved, relationships restored, addictions broken, sicknesses healed, and so many more.

This works better than any kind of spiritual warfare praying I had ever conducted in the past.

It can work for you too.

# CHAPTER 8:

# JUSTICE AND THE COURTS OF HEAVEN IN THE BIBLE

---

HOW TO DO SPIRITUAL WARFARE THE RIGHT WAY

BY GREG KURJATA

It's one thing to flash a few scriptures and share a few testimonies, and quite another to show where this process has been in place since the beginning of time. I'm going to attempt to show you biblical proof of where in the history of mankind the use of judgements, justice, judges and courts have been connected to great battles that were won by the Lord.

The first one we'll look at is in the book of Judges. This is a bit of a lengthy passage but I need to include the entire passage for context. I have bolded the passages that I want you to pay attention to:

### Judges 2:10-18

**10** When that entire generation had been gathered to their ancestors, another generation arose **that knew neither Adonai nor the work he had done for Isra'el. 11 Then the people of Isra'el did what was evil from Adonai's perspective and served the ba'alim. 12 They abandoned Adonai, the God of their fathers,** who had brought them out of the land of Egypt, and followed other gods, selected from the gods of the peoples around them, and worshipped them; this made Adonai angry. **13 They abandoned Adonai and served Ba'al and the 'ashtarot. 14** The anger of Adonai blazed against Isra'el; and he handed them over to pillagers, who plundered them, and to their enemies around them; so that they could no longer resist their enemies. **15** Whenever they launched an attack, the power of Adonai was against them, so that things turned out badly — just as Adonai had said would happen and had sworn to them. **They were in dire distress.**

*Judges*

**16 But then Adonai raised up judges, who rescued them from the power of those who were plundering them. 17** Yet they did not pay attention to their judges, but made whores of themselves to other gods and worshipped them; they quickly turned away from the path on which their ancestors had walked, the way of obeying Adonai's mitzvot — they failed to do this. **18 When Adonai raised up judges for them, Adonai was with the judge and delivered them from the hands of their enemies throughout the lifetime of the judge; for Adonai was moved to pity by their groaning under those oppressing and crushing them.**

Read the entire second chapter of Judges. It starts with the Angel of the Lord rebuking the entire nation for not doing what the Lord had commanded them to do in driving out the nations in the land. Then it tracks the story forward in history about 120 years once each generation of those who were brought into the promised land were now dead.

## GOD RAISED UP JUDGES

Then, a generation arose that did not know either God or His works. The entire nation turned away from God and served the idols and demons of the nations they failed to drive out from the land. This brought the nation of Israel into a state of dire distress. Now pay close attention to what God did:

He raised up judges.

He didn't raise up a king.

He raised up judges.

## THE SHADOW OF THE LORD (*Principle*)

Here's why. There is a principle in scripture called the Shadow of the Lord.

I won't go fully into it here for the sake of time, but it has to do with the making of a heavenly reality on earth as it is in heaven. Moses was told to build the tabernacle exactly like what he was shown in the mountain. (Heb 8) When He did, the glory of the Lord manifested on the tabernacle. The tabernacle on earth became like what it is in heaven.

*on earth like it is in Heaven*

Or Jesus being the Word made flesh and dwelling among us (John 1:14) - and the glory and Spirit of God resting upon Him. Heaven's reality was surrounding Jesus everywhere he went.

This is what we want to help you achieve in your spiritual walk with God. To walk together with you and bring you into the experience and the encounter of the glory of God in such a way that you become the shadow of the Lord upon the earth. If this is something you would like, become a part of our community by joining the JCH Online Student Group: https://jchonline.ca/jchcourse

Psalm 91:1-2 NIV says this:

"Whoever dwells in the shelter of the Most High will rest in the shadow of the Almighty. 2 I will say of the Lord, "He is my refuge and my fortress, my God, in whom I trust."

There isn't a light that is greater than God. Meaning that the shadow of God has nothing to do with the light shining behind him. What it means is; as we abide in the shelter of the most high that the very image and likeness of who he is, is imprinted into our spirit and soul, our heart and our body, then we carry the image of God on the earth.

What this means to the issue of courts and judges is this: judges are God's idea and the way that He would rule a nation. He calls Himself a Judge of everyone (Heb 12:22). When Judges function according to God's plan on earth, then the heavenly reality of what they represent has an opportunity to manifest and bring blessing to all who are in contact with it.

Judges and courts are a design from heaven. It is the place where justice is delivered. We have an imperfect system on earth. That's why I encourage people every chance I get to pray for the judges in the land, as they are God's representatives for justice. If they are just - blessing can be released. If they are corrupt - then curses are released. The more we pray for the best judges to be appointed, the more good judges will be appointed. I've witnessed this first hand in my province.

Judges 2:16 says:

> **16 But then Adonai raised up judges, who rescued them from the power of those who were plundering them.**

The way that God dealt with His people being plundered was through judges. They would judge the people of Israel first, then go to battle. In this way the nation of Israel was delivered from their enemies, until they went back to their idol worship. Then God had to do it again. And again. And again.

Judge
Go to battle

## OTNIEL

In Judges 3 the bible begins to detail some of the exploits of the judges.

### Judges 3:9-11

9 But when the people of Isra'el cried out to *Adonai*, *Adonai* raised up a savior for the people of Isra'el; and he rescued them; this was 'Otni'el, the son of Kalev's younger brother K'naz. **10 The spirit of *Adonai* came upon him, and he judged Isra'el. Then he went out to war,** and *Adonai* gave Kushan-Rish'atayim king of Aram into his hands; his power prevailed against Kushan-Rish'atayim. 11 So the land had rest for forty years, until 'Otni'el the son of K'naz died.

See the pattern:

1. Spirit of the Lord came upon him
2. He judged Israel
3. Then he went to war.

*Pattern of spiritual Warfare*

This is one of the patterns of spiritual warfare in the bible. It is done through the courts via a judgement of some kind. When they followed this pattern they had peace. *old Test*

In Judges 4 the bible introduces Deborah, one of the great judges of Israel.

**D'vorah**

### Judges 4:4

4 Now D'vorah, a woman and a prophet, the wife of Lapidot, **was judging Isra'el at that time. 5** She used to sit under D'vorah's Palm between Ramah and Beit-El, in the hills of Efrayim; **and the people of Isra'el would come to her for judgment.**

You can read the rest of the story in Judges, but Deborah delivered the nation by justice and her faith in God. She was a prophet AND a judge. She judged first, then they went to battle.

## SAMUEL

Another supernatural deliverance that happened for Israel was in the days of Samuel the prophet.

Again, I have highlighted the areas I want to emphasize.

### 1 Samuel 7:5-14

5 Sh'mu'el said, "Gather all Isra'el to Mitzpah, and I will pray for you to Adonai." 6 So they gathered together at Mitzpah, drew water and poured it out before Adonai, fasted that day, and said there, "We have sinned against Adonai." **Sh'mu'el began serving as judge over the people of Isra'el at Mitzpah.**

7 When the P'lishtim heard that the people of Isra'el had gathered together at Mitzpah, the leaders of the P'lishtim marched up against Isra'el; and when the people of Isra'el heard about this, they were afraid of the P'lishtim. 8 The people of Isra'el said to Sh'mu'el, "Don't stop crying out to Adonai our God for us, to save us from the power of the P'lishtim." 9 Sh'mu'el took a baby lamb and offered it as a whole burnt offering to Adonai. **Then Sh'mu'el cried to Adonai for Isra'el, and Adonai answered him. 10 As Sh'mu'el was presenting the burnt offering, the P'lishtim advanced to attack Isra'el. But this time, Adonai thundered violently over the P'lishtim, throwing them into such confusion that they were struck down before Isra'el. 11 The**

men of Isra'el went out from Mitzpah, pursuing the P'lishtim and attacking them all the way to Beit-Kar.

**12** Sh'mu'el took a stone, placed it between Mitzpah and Shen, and gave it the name Even-'Ezer [stone of help], explaining, "Adonai has helped us until now." **13** Thus the P'lishtim were humbled, so that they no longer entered Isra'el's territory; and the hand of Adonai was against the P'lishtim as long as Sh'mu'el lived. **14 The cities between 'Ekron and Gat which the P'lishtim had captured from Isra'el were restored to Isra'el, and Isra'el rescued all this territory from the power of the P'lishtim. There was also peace between Isra'el and the Emori.**

Here's what I want you to pay attention to:

1. The nation of Israel had decided to turn back to God with their whole heart. Samuel had made that a condition of him becoming a judge for them.

2. He gathered them at MITZPAH - this means a pillar of covenant. The first mention in scripture was when Jacob made a covenant with Laban and the pillar was named Mitzpah - with the words - The Lord is witness of our covenant.

3. Samuel judges the nation.

4. Samuel cries out to the Lord when he sees the enemy attacking.

5. The Lord fights the battle and the enemy is defeated supernaturally.

6. The enemy has to return territory that they had plundered.

7. Even their other enemies lived at peace with them.

What is being demonstrated is the relationship between judges and successful battle. Spiritual warfare must be conducted this way - legally first.

Each of these references follows a pattern. It was through justice that God brought deliverance to the people of Israel. The pattern with them was they needed to come back to God and put away their idols. Once they did that then God could move on their behalf.

When you want justice in the same way that God does then you will witness His creative power move on your behalf.

Come back to God
Put away idols

God could move ...

when you want
justice the way God
does — witness His
creative power to
move on your behalf.

relationship between
Judges &
Successful battles.

Spiritual warfare must
be conducted this way —
Legally first!

It was through justice
that God brought
deliverance to people of
Israel!

# CHAPTER 9:

# USE THIS SPIRITUAL WARFARE PRAYER TEMPLATE - IT WORKED FOR HIM, IT'LL WORK FOR YOU

---

## HOW TO DO SPIRITUAL WARFARE THE RIGHT WAY

### BY GREG KURJATA

Now this story is one of my favourites.

Y'hoshafat was a good king who followed God with his whole heart, for the most part. He had some slip ups but that's for another story. In 2 Chronicles 19, he makes it his life's work to bring the nation back to God and to appoint judges in the land.

This is key to understand how this king thought. He came by it honestly because his name means the Lord is Judge. He knew that having righteous judges in the land would enable the voice of God to be accessible in the everyday affairs of the communities the judges presided over. If the judges feared God, then God would help them make the appropriate decisions in each case.

Y'hosahafat valued justice. I believe he took the action that he did because he knew it pleased God. It seems that when biblical leaders recognized the very heart and passion of God, that justice was a part of what they executed upon the earth. So what he did in 2 Chronicles 19 lays the foundation for what happened in chapter 20 as you will see.

## THE ATTACK ON JUDAH

2 Chronicles 20 begins with a real problem. It seemed that even though the entire nation was returning to God, their enemies were getting ready to attack them. There's a number of places in the Bible that seem to indicate that the adversary may have advanced knowledge of what God is about to do. In this case the nation was coming back to God. In the case of the birth of Moses, the adversary tried to kill all the boys that were two years old and younger. The same happened with Jesus.

Whatever the case may be, the nation of Judah was being attacked without just cause.

### 2 Chronicles 20:1-4

Some time later, the people of Mo'av and the people of 'Amon with other 'Amonim came up to fight Y'hoshafat. **2** Y'hoshafat was told, "A huge army from beyond the [Dead] Sea, from Aram, is on its way to fight you; right now they are in Hatzatzon-Tamar" (that is, 'Ein-Gedi). **3** Y'hoshafat was frightened, so he determined to seek Adonai. He proclaimed a fast throughout all Y'hudah, **4** and Y'hudah assembled to seek help from Adonai; they came from all the cities of Y'hudah to seek Adonai.

I cover this prayer in detail on Day 1 of our monthly 5 Day Salvation Challenge, where we equip people to pray for the salvation of their lost love ones by using the Courts Of Heaven. This prayer is a template we use for making our petition for the salvation of our loved ones on Day 5 in the Courts of Heaven. www.jchonline.ca/5dsc

The people did the right thing. They were alarmed that their enemies were gathering to attack and took measures to do something about it. Because the enemy armies were too great, they knew their only hope was to get help from the Lord Himself.

### 2 Chronicles 20:5-12

**5** Standing in front of the new courtyard in the house of *Adonai*, among those assembled from Y'hudah and Yerushalayim, **6** he said: "*Adonai*, God of our ancestors, you alone are God in heaven. You rule all the kingdoms of the nations. In your hand are power and strength, so that no one can withstand you. **7** You, our God, drove out those living in the land ahead of your people Isra'el and gave it forever to the descendants of Avraham your friend. **8** They lived in it, built you a sanctuary in it **for your name**, and said, **9** 'If calamity strikes us, such as war, judgment, disease or famine, **we will stand before this house — that is, before you, since your name is in this house** — and cry to you in our distress; and you will hear us and rescue us.'

**10** "So now, see: the people of 'Amon, Mo'av and Mount Se'ir, whom you would not let Isra'el invade when they came out of the land of Egypt, so that they turned away from them and did not destroy them, **11** are now repaying us [evil]; they have come to throw us out of your possession, which you gave us as an inheritance. **12 Our God! Won't you execute judgment against them?** For we haven't strength enough to defeat this huge horde coming against us, and we don't know what to do, but our eyes are on you."

*Wow*

**The ONLY question in his prayer was WON'T YOU EXECUTE JUDGMENT AGAINST THEM?**

Wow!

He knew God was judge and that God would rule in His favour against his enemies. But he asked for something very powerful that we teach in depth in our course - he asked for the judgment to be executed.

*Judgement to be Executed*

This is the same thing that the widow woman from Luke 18 asked the unjust judge. She knew a judgment from the court would end her problem. I believe Jehoshaphat had the same idea in his mind, that a judgment from the court of heaven would end their problem.

*Name of the Lord*

The other item I would like to point out is that the name of the Lord was in the temple of Solomon. His understanding of the name of the Lord revealed that he was praying in the presence of the name. As they were praying before this temple they were understanding they were praying before the name of the Lord. Where the name of the Lord is the presence of God is.

In our time where the name of Jesus is the presence of the Lord is. In a couple of minutes we're going to look at the function of the right hand of God and how all of this works together right now in our day and time.

Back to the story.

The enemy gathers to attack, the nation gathers to pray, the king asks that God would execute judgments against their enemies.

What happens next is pure adventure of biblical proportions.

As they are praying and looking to God for direction, the Spirit of the Lord inspires a prophet in their assembly to give a very detailed prophecy of where to find the enemy, what to do when they found them, and ends with a "kicking butt and taking names" statement from heaven, *Haha!*

*God shows them the where enemy is*

**2 Chronicles 20:15-17 NIV**

**15** He said: "Listen, King Jehoshaphat and all who live in Judah and Jerusalem! This is what the Lord says to you: 'Do not be afraid or discouraged because of this vast army. **For the battle is not yours, but God's. 16** Tomorrow march down against them. They will be climbing up by the Pass of Ziz, and you will find them at the end of the gorge in the Desert of Jeruel. **17 You will not have to fight this battle.** Take up your positions; **stand firm and see the deliverance**

*HS: Some = He reveals the enemies Sceners and Footholds*

**the Lord will give you**, Judah and Jerusalem. Do not be afraid; do not be discouraged. **Go out to face them tomorrow, and the Lord will be with you.'"**

Here's a breakdown of this prophetic word.

First of all, God made it very clear that this was his battle to fight. Jehoshaphat asked that he would execute judgment against his enemies, and God was going to do exactly that. There's a popular worship song that says God is going to fight your battles. That is absolutely true. But if you want to be biblical about it, it's in the context of justice that God fights your battle. He does it legally by issuing a ruling in your favour. That is how he fights your battles.

Next the Holy Spirit provided a battle strategy by revealing where the enemy had gathered and what Judah was supposed to do when they got to the battlefield. He told them to show up.

Next he reiterates that he is going to fight the battle, and that they would see the deliverance of the Lord. Finally he closes it with an encouragement for them not to be afraid or dismayed and that he was with them.

At this point the worship team broke out in praise at the top of their voices and the entire assembly was encouraged by the word of the Lord. Here's what happened next:

### 2 Chronicles 20:20-21

**20** The next morning, they rose early and went out into the T'koa Desert. As they left, Y'hoshafat stood and said, "Listen to me, Y'hudah and you inhabitants of Yerushalayim!

> **"Trust in Adonai your God,**
> **and you will be safe.**
> **Trust in his prophets,**
> **and you will succeed."**
> **21 After consulting with the people, he appointed those**
> **who would sing to Adonai and praise the splendor of his**
> **holiness** as they went out ahead of the army, saying, "Give
> thanks to Adonai, for his grace continues forever."

The wisdom Y'hoshafat carried was remarkable. He continued to
encourage the people to not only trust God but to trust the prophets
who were the spokespersons for God. Meaning - trust not only in the
Lord but trust His Word and succeed.

Perhaps the most unusual warfare tactic ever used was conducted
in this battle set up. Y'hoshafat asks the people about appointing a
choir to lead into battle. They all thought it was a good idea, in light of
the Word of the Lord to them related to how God was going to fight
their battle, and all they would need to do is stand still and see what
God would do.

So the musicians are singing to the Lord as they go to the place
the enemy is, and here's what happened to their enemy:

#### 2 Chronicles 20:22-26

**22** Then, during the time when they were singing and
praising, Adonai brought a surprise attack against the people
of 'Amon, Mo'av and Mount Se'ir who had come to fight
Y'hudah; and they were defeated. **23** What happened was
that the people of 'Amon and Mo'av began attacking those
people who lived by Mount Se'ir, **to kill and destroy them**

*Attack each other*

completely*; and when they had finished off the people from Se'ir, they set to work slaughtering one another. 24* So when Y'hudah reached the watchtower overlooking the desert, they looked toward the horde; and there in front of them were corpses fallen to the ground; **none had escaped.** **25** Y'hoshafat and his army came to take the spoil from them and found among them personal property in abundance and corpses with precious jewels, which they stripped off for themselves until they couldn't carry any more. **They took three days just to collect the spoil, there was so much. 26** On the fourth day, they assembled in the Valley of B'rakhah [blessing], where they blessed Adonai; hence that place is called the Valley of B'rakhah to this day.

*Spoils – 3 days to gather*

What started as an impossible situation, ended with three days of gathering the spoil. It began as a day of devastation, and ended as a day of blessing. There was no chance for backlash from the adversary. The judgment from the court of heaven was the answer to the problem.

For years I heard various messages, and even preached a few myself, using this passage to demonstrate the value of praise and worship. The focus has always been on how when they began to sing to the Lord the enemy was defeated.

Without question, praise is a powerful weapon to bring light into dark places. But what never gets talked about is how Y'hoshafat asked God to execute judgment against his enemies. That was the secret sauce to this entire miracle.

*No Chance for Backlash* — *yes!*

## THIS BATTLE WAS WON LEGALLY FIRST

They had a ruling from the court in the form of the prophecy that was delivered. It outlined what was going to happen in the favour of Y'hoshafat and Y'hudah. Once they had the ruling, the praise began. The praise was the response to the Word of the Lord which in this case was the actual ruling from heaven in answer to the question of executing judgment on their enemies.

Can you now see how justice and spiritual warfare are intricately connected?

In the book of Daniel nothing happened against the enemy until the court went into session. In 2 Chronicles chapter 20 the enemy was defeated after God executed judgment against them. The widow woman had her victory as soon as she got justice from the judge.

All three are actions of the court.

*Go to Court —*

*Get a ruling*

Battle won !
legally First !

~~~~~~~~~~~~

Ruling from the Ct

# CHAPTER 10:

# THE THRONE IS THE FOCUS

---

In our course we have 2 sessions on the various courts that are in the bible, where to find them, and what their function is. One of those courts is found in Revelation 4.

I mentioned earlier that as I researched the bible to understand what the Holy Spirit had shown me, I found that wherever a throne was mentioned in a vision (theophany for us bible nerds) it was the location of a court. This holds especially true of Revelation 4-6.

I'm not going to go into all of details around the passage, but I *Ruling* will focus on how Jesus was involved in a heavenly court ruling and *Execution* execution. And if he is doing things like this in the invisible realm, the heavenly realm, then we can expect to be able to do the same thing.

In John 14:12, Jesus said, "the works that I do you shall do also, and greater works than these shall you do because I go to the Father."

I believe what you are about to see is part of the greater works that Jesus said we would be able to do because he goes to the Father.

### Revelation 4:1-3

After these things, I looked; and there before me was a door standing open in heaven; and the voice like a trumpet which I had heard speaking with me before said, "**Come up here, and I will show you** what must happen after these things." **2 Instantly I was in the Spirit**, and there before me **in heaven stood a throne**, and **on the throne** Someone was sitting.

One of our specialties is that we teach how to see in the spirit and get yourself positioned to be invited by the Spirit of God into these heavenly places. This is a reality that still exists and is available to every person alive.

We can see into the heavenly places

I say that to underline that this heavenly court is in a heavenly place. If you are not used to seeing spiritually you're missing out on so much adventure and knowledge of God.

John was in a vision and saw a door open in heaven. That means there are doors in heavenly places that are transition points for human beings.

John saw one of these doors. He was invited into that realm with these words, "Come up here, and I will show you what must happen..." Up is better than down. He was invited into a higher realm than the one he was currently existing within. It's more of a dimension shift than a going up into the sky.

Jesus had said that the kingdom of heaven is at hand, meaning it's within reach and easily accessible. Earlier on in this book I mentioned how even children could enter the kingdom of heaven. If children can enter the kingdom of heaven then anyone can. Stepping into the heavenly realm is an action of faith.

As soon as he responded to the invitation he was in the spirit. Verse 2 says it this way,

*Instantly*

"**2 Instantly I was in the SPIRIT**, and there before me **in HEAVEN stood a throne...**"

*No waiting*

According to John, being in the spirit and in heaven are the same thing. When he was in the spirit he could see the heavenly realm.

Notice in the next section of this passage in scripture, that what is being described by John, is being described in relation to the throne, starting with the One Who is seated on the Throne. Even though He is the Lord Almighty, in this vision, He is not the subject of the vision - the throne is along with the effect of the throne on what is happening. I've bolded the references to the throne.

### Revelation 4:2b-8

...and **on the throne** Someone was sitting.

3 The One sitting there gleamed like diamonds and rubies, and a rainbow shining like emerald **encircled the throne**.

4 **Surrounding the throne** were twenty-four other thrones, and on the thrones sat twenty-four elders dressed in white clothing and wearing gold crowns on their heads. 5 **From the throne** came forth lightnings, voices and thunderings; and **before the throne** were seven flaming torches, which are the sevenfold Spirit of God. 6 **In front of the throne** was what looked like a sea of glass, clear as crystal. **In the center, around the throne**, were four living beings covered with eyes in front and behind. 7 The first living being was like a lion, the second living being was like an ox, the third living being had a face that looked human, and the fourth living being was like a flying eagle.[a] 8 Each of the four living beings had six wings[b] and was covered with eyes inside and out; and day and night they never stop saying,

"Holy, holy, holy is Adonai, God of heaven's armies[c] the One who was, who is and who is coming!"

I'm not going to go into detail of what each element means, it's in the course in the sessions on the various courts. All of it matters and is vitally important to understand, and some of it is not what you might think.

Now look at how many times the throne is mentioned.

1.  on the throne
2.  encircled the throne
3.  surrounding the throne

4. from the throne

5. before the throne

6. in front of the throne

7. in the centre around the throne

Seven times the throne is mentioned.

Seven in Hebrew is zayin. It has several meanings such as straight light from God to Man, or returning light. It can also mean sword and nourishment at the same time. It's used as a time divider as in 7 days in a week, 7 X 7 = 49 for sha'vuot etc. One postulation is that it is Jesus the crowned Man because of what zayin looks like as an aleph-biet character. Some have said it is the number of perfection or completion. It is mentioned 860 times in the bible.

If we prophetically combine the meanings of zayin - like assembling a puzzle, you could say this:

*...that the justice of the throne of God returns His light to man directly, and each ruling contains the sword of judgment against the enemy, and the nourishment of favour in the same ruling to humanity.*

I have to say - that's a pretty good thing to have happen as a definition of the number 7 and the throne.

This place is the Supreme Court of Heaven. It is the epicentre of the justice of God. Each reference to the throne, the beings, colours, and elements have function and meaning. In fact their function ascribes their meaning.

This court has been in session because of what happens in verse 1 of chapter 5.

**Revelation 5:1-2**

**Next I saw in the right hand of the One sitting on the throne**
**a scroll with writing on both sides and sealed with seven**
**seals**; **2** and I saw a mighty angel proclaiming in a loud voice,
"Who is worthy to open the scroll and break its seals?

The One sitting on the throne has a scroll in his right hand. The
scroll is the ruling of the Supreme Court of Heaven. The Bible doesn't
mention when the court deliberated or how a ruling was determined.
But we see the Father is holding it in His right hand. There's a reason
for that. I mentioned earlier in a parenthetical statement that the
right hand of God is a function not a position or place.

If you know your bible you will know that we are raised up and
seated with Jesus in the heavenly places, at the right hand of God. The
problem is this - there is only one throne. There are not 2 thrones
side by side mentioned in the bible - meaning the Father has a throne,
then Jesus has His throne at the right hand of the Father's throne.

It **does mention** that Jesus and the Father are in the same throne.

## THE PATH OF THE RULING

*Hebrew Function not Form*

The only way to understand this is by looking at it the way a Hebrew
would. By Function not Form.

The right hand of God is a function. It is not a chair beside the
throne of God. Jesus demonstrates the function of the right hand of
God in chapter 5 and 6 of Revelation.

In Revelation 5, Jesus is found to be worthy to open the scroll and
read its contents.

*Jesus opens the scroll*

### Revelation 5:7

**7** He came and **took the scroll out of the right hand of the One sitting on the throne**.

Once he takes possession of this ruling that the Judge had in his right hand, Jesus becomes responsible for what happens with the ruling.

Jesus is then worshiped as God, because he has all authority and power, represented by the details of verse 6. In fact all of creation worships Him and one of the greatest worship sessions recorded in the bible happens.

Remember I mentioned during the story of Y'hoshaphat that things changed in the new covenant regarding the execution of the judgements of God. This event is an example of that very thing.

### Revelation 6:1-2

**Next I watched as the Lamb broke the first of the seven seals**, and I heard one of the four living beings say in a thundering voice, 'Go!' **2** I looked, and there in front of me was a white horse; its rider had a bow and was given a crown; and he rode off as a conqueror to conquer.

What Jesus did in this verse is show us how to function in the right hand of God. I call it the *Path of the Ruling*.

**The right hand of God has the function of executing the will of the One on the throne, and any of the rulings of that throne.**

Throughout the bible the right hand of God represents the executive authority of the Lord.

We are in Him and share in His authority and Name. Our function as the Body of Christ is now similar to His. We also have the right and power to execute the rulings of the courts of heaven. In fact, this is what standing in the name of Jesus means. It is an executive function.

*Seal Must be broken*

Notice that <u>NOTHING HAPPENS *UNTIL* JESUS BREAKS A</u>
<u>SEAL ON THE RULING</u> of the court.

As soon as He begins the process of execution, all of the judgements
of God are released and events start to unfold.

I am hoping that you see the raw power of this. The implications
are astounding to realize that God wants to partner with you to this
same extent.

You are in Jesus on the earth. You carry His name among
humanity.

*God Partner*

Over the past couple of years I have invested 10's of
thousands of dollars into courses, coaching and consultants,
to develop myself and my businesses. It is the best use of funds
I can think of. Specialized knowledge is valuable because it
targets the area of growth and development with a laser-
like accuracy. <u>Investment into your spiritual life is equally</u>
<u>important</u> - like books, study guides, courses, coaching and
community memberships. When investment is made in this
way, <u>the value of it is multiplied in your heart</u>. It costs you
something. And when it costs you something, <u>the chances
are very high that you will take action on the information
provided.</u> Plus, it is laser targeted for a very specific result.

We specialize in helping people grow to a maturity in the
heavenly realm where you can function at a very high level
of authority and power, and have two feet on the ground at
the same time. If you have not yet done so, Join our Student
Group today.

https://www.jchonline.ca/jchcourse

*we function as Jesus does*

You have a function, and part of that function is to do what Jesus does.

Jesus executes the rulings of the Courts Of Heaven.

In John 14:12 He told His disciples this:

### John 14:12-13

12 Yes, indeed! I tell you that whoever trusts in me will also do the works I do! **Indeed, he will do greater ones, because I am going to the Father.** 13 In fact, whatever you ask for in my name, I will do; so that the Father may be glorified in the Son. 14 If you ask me for something in my name, I will do it.

The fact that Jesus has gone *TO* the Father is the reason why we can expect to do greater works that encompass not only the works that He did in the Gospels, but those that He accomplished in the book of Revelation. In fact, I'll go so far as to say that whatever He does in Revelation would be done in partnership with someone or a group of people that are His followers on earth.

Here's a couple more references for you, to show how warfare and justice are connected.

In Revelation 15 and 16, you see the seven golden bowls that are being released from the scroll that Jesus was executing. Look at what happened with one of the bowls being poured out:

### Revelation 16:10

10 The fifth one **poured out his bowl on the throne of the beast, and its kingdom grew dark**. People gnawed on their tongues from the pain, 11 yet they cursed the God of heaven because of their pains and sores, and did not turn from their sinful deeds.

When this judgement was executed against the throne of the beast, any human person attached to that throne suffered terribly. This holds true today. When God judges something in the dark spirit world, any person attached to that thing will be impacted by their connection to it.

The connection of throne and kingdom also needs to be recognized here. The throne of God is the centre of His Kingdom. Any person attached to His throne enjoys the blessing of being connected to life.

Then there's this: The final end of Lucifer, the adversary...

### Revelation 20:1-4a

Next I saw an angel coming down from heaven, who had the key to the Abyss and a great chain in his hand. **2** He seized the dragon, that ancient serpent, who is the Devil and Satan [the Adversary], and chained him up for a thousand years. **3** He threw him into the Abyss, locked it and sealed it over him; so that he could not deceive the nations any more until the thousand years were over. After that, he has to be set free for a little while.

**4 Then I saw thrones, and those seated on them received authority to judge.**

I wonder who this nameless angel is? Apparently this angel was given or is responsible for the key to the Abyss and packs a great chain. I have no idea what his name might be, but have called him Leroy - the most unlikely angel to be selected to the ball team - Leroy. The guy who no one paid attention to, and quietly went about his work without fanfare or being noticed. That's the guy that God picks to lock up the enemy of all humanity. Leroy - the nameless angel. He humbled himself and was exalted to accomplish a powerful task to the benefit of the Kingdom of Heaven.

Once the devil is locked up, a phenomenon happens… thrones are seen, and **there are people sitting on those thrones** who were given authority to judge.

Where did these thrones come from? Who are the people sitting on these thrones?

I have a theory: I think the people on these thrones were connected to the locking up of satan, the devil, the dragon, and the ancient serpent. The fact that they were given authority to judge means that they did something to merit that type of promotion. I think they were the authority of God released on the earth to effect that event. It has not happened yet - but it will.

Maybe you, or I, or both of us will be found on those thrones to bring an end to the works of the devil.

Well, there you go.

I have shown you throughout the bible how justice and warfare are connected and how God will still use the same processes today, if we will only trust Him enough to act on what the bible is showing us to do.

Doing spiritual warfare the right way is doing the warfare legally through the courts of heaven, then going to battle with the rulings and judgements of the court.

Imagine your life without counter-attacks and backlash.

It is possible for you to enjoy this kind of existence, and to be extremely effective at bringing heaven to earth in your world.

## WHAT KIND OF SPIRITUAL WARFARE PRAYER
## SHOULD YOU PRAY?

There isn't a simple answer for this, nor is it possible to provide a 'sample prayer' for you to pray - other than the template from Jehoshaphat - because every situation is so uniquely different. You can adapt his prayer template to suit your own individual situation. Approach it like an experiment to see how it works. As you continue to use the prayer template, and you see the results, you'll gain your own experience by simply putting in the reps.

If you are interested in more advanced spiritual warfare prayer strategies, we have created an Advanced Prayer Strategies Workshop. You may have already purchased this workshop when you bought the book. If you haven't you can get it here: https://www.jchonline.ca/apsw-swf

The workshop provides scriptural foundation and then specific examples of prayers in different areas of life. You'll learn how to deal with generational curses, blood oaths, generational traumas, spiritual agreements, justice for your DNA, and much more.

The best way to learn this information is in a workshop/course format. This way you can see, hear and interact with the information at a different level than in a book.

Plus you'll see the prayers, along with the attitude within the prayers, when they are prayed. Some things are better caught than taught. There will be insight that you'll receive from observing how it's done rather than trying to figure it out for yourself and wondering if you're doing it right.

Our online course is 14 hours long. There's an important reason for that; you need depth in the word of God, and maturity as a son or daughter of God to be effective in this kind of praying.

What you've learned in this book gives you a starting point for understanding how the courts of heaven are used to conduct spiritual warfare. But there's much more to know in order to be effective at spiritual warfare through the Courts Of Heaven. Adding this skill to your life will expand your effectiveness in prayer.

Listen, it took me over 10 years to get to where I felt confident that I would be able to share this information in an easy to understand and workable format. We take very complex concepts and make them simple to understand so they can activate in every day life.

I have a saying that if it doesn't work in shoe leather I'm not interested in doing it. Meaning, it has to make sense and be useful when I'm going shopping, when I'm cooking a meal, when I'm taking a walk, when I'm doing work of any kind, when I'm having a conversation with a friend. If what I teach doesn't make sense in ordinary moments of life then I'm not interested in talking about it. What I am interested in is helping to release you into the fullness of what God has created you for.

# CHAPTER 11:
# WHAT YOU NEED TO DO NEXT...

———

## HOW TO DO SPIRITUAL WARFARE THE RIGHT WAY

BY GREG KURJATA

The most important thing that you could do right away is to take action. In James 1 it says if anyone is a hearer of the word and not a doer he deceives his own heart. It's important that you take action on what you've learned in this book.

The first thing I suggest that you do is go through the **Advanced Prayer Strategies Workshop**. Especially if this information is new to you. (You may already have this in your membership area if you purchased it along with the book.)

It's going to be different than what you're used to hearing and seeing in a prayer workshop. Of course it's 100% Bible. What makes it different is we come at it from a heaven to earth perspective.

Then... find your tribe.

You want to be around people that are on the same path and on the same trajectory as you are. A lot of things can be worked out in your own private time within your own heart, and that personal development is very important. But when you can find fellowship with like-minded people there's a synergy that takes place that is encouraging.

There are several ways that you can connect with us:

1. **Join our free Five Day Salvation Challenge**.

In this challenge you will learn a prayer strategy that has worked for thousands of people who have prayed for their loved ones to come to Jesus. Over 90,000 passionate followers of Jesus have taken the challenge and thousands have seen their loved ones come to Christ.

2. **Enroll as a student in the JCH Online Course.**

Over 2300 students (as of this edit) have enrolled in our online course. You can see some of their comments and testimonies when you click the link. It is a comprehensive discovery of the Courts Of Heaven throughout the Bible. You get over 14 hours of training in 54 videos, with downloadable MP3 and PDF notes. PLUS over $200 in bonus materials as an ethical bribe to entice you to join our student group. We want you to know, you would be our favourite. :)

Visit www.jchonline.ca/jchcourse

**3. Take the God First Process On Demand Intensive.**

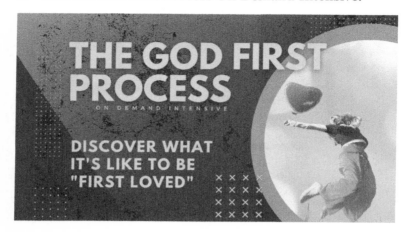

This process connects you with the love and power of God quicker than anything I know. It's the breakthrough you've been praying for. Get to know God in a whole new level by learning and practising the God First Process

www.jchonline.ca/godfirst

**4. Join us live online for our weekly JCH Online Broadcasts.**

Every Thursday and Sunday at 3 PM mountain time we have our JCH online broadcast. On Sundays we focus on healing and on Thursdays we teach a series, have guests, and often do activations and pray for the sick as well. It's an international community. God has been moving in great power of signs, wonders and miracles.

To join through **FACEBOOK:**

www.facebook.com/justiceandthecourtsofheaven

To join through **YOUTUBE:**

www.youtube.com/courtsofheaven

**5. Book a One on One Session With Greg.**

There are 2 reasons why people want to book a session with me: 1. they have an urgent situation that needs an immediate answer from heaven and results from the Courts of Heaven. 2. They are stuck, sick, or oppressed in some way, and have done many things to get set free. Our prayer process during a session has helped hundreds of people find what they were seeking.

Go to www.jchonline.ca/one to learn more.

# ABOUT THE AUTHOR

Greg is a son of God, a husband, a dad, a brother, an uncle, a teacher, a pastor, an author, an entrepreneur, a musician, and a super nacho maker.

His life mission has always been to help people discover and passionately follow Jesus.

He has been involved in every level of church ministry from being a worship leader, small group leader, youth pastor, lead pastor, national board member, evangelism director, missionary, tech team leader, manly coffee maker and chair stacker.

Along with his wife Val, they have built the JCH Online Community by hosting monthly 5 Day Salvation Challenges, weekly broadcasts, and special prayer events.

They have 2 married daughters who assist in the online community and provide endless moral support.

You can reach him by email at: support@courtsofheaven.ca

JCH Online stands for Justice and the Courts of Heaven Online. Our online presence include various social media platforms such as Facebook, Youtube, Instagram and TikTok.

Made in United States
Orlando, FL
15 February 2023

30038371R10071